little bits of ruined beauty

by **Tom Wentworth**

Little Bits of Ruined Beauty was first performed at Pentabus Theatre, Bromfield, Shropshire, on Thursday 29 September 2022.

little bits of ruined beauty

by **Tom Wentworth**

Cast

Terry Lynham	Nigel Barrett
Eddie Lynham	Joseph Brown

Creative Team

Director	Nickie Miles-Wildin
Designer	Rachana Jadhav
Lighting Designer	James Mackenzie
Sound Design & Composition	Charlotte Barber
Video Design & Captions	Ben Glover
Dramaturg	Stephanie Dale
Voice & Accent Coach	Natalie Grady
Movement Director	Lizzie Wiggs
Access Consultant	Chloë Clarke
Access & Engagement Consultant & Facilitator	Alex Whiteley
Production Manager	Keith Tunstill
Stage Manager – Rehearsals	Jessica Chaplin
Touring Stage Manager	Miranda Lowe

Produced by Pentabus. Commissioned and supported by Unlimited, celebrating the work of disabled artists, with funding from Arts Council England and Paul Hamlyn Foundation.

Special Thanks to:

Joseph Alessi, The Belgrade Theatre, Tim Brierley, Adam Fenton, Kate Hall, Will Hall, Lois Hopwood, Sophie Motley.

Tour Dates

Thursday 29 September | Pentabus | Shropshire
Friday 30 September | Pentabus | Shropshire
Saturday 1 October | Quatt Village Hall | Shropshire

Monday 3 October | Hereford College of Arts | Herefordshire
Tuesday 4 October | Theatr Brycheiniog | Powys
Wednesday 5 October | Theatr Brycheiniog | Powys

Wednesday 12 October | Aberystwyth Arts Centre | Ceredigion
Saturday 15 October | Ludlow Assembly Rooms | Shropshire
Sunday 16 October | Theatre Severn | Shropshire

Thursday 20 October | Knighton Community Centre | Powys

Cast

Nigel Barrett | Terry

Theatre credits include: *Britannicus* (Lyric Hammersmith); *I Am Kevin, 100: Unearthed* (Wildworks); *Pops* (Edinburgh/High Tide Festival); *The Show in Which Hopefully Nothing Happens, Baddies the Musical* (Unicorn); *The Mysteries* (Royal Exchange Manchester); *Party Skills For The End of The World* (Manchester International Festival/Shoreditch Town Hall); *Kingdom Come, Richard III – An Arab Tragedy* (RSC); *Margate/Dreamland* (Shoreditch Town Hall); *Blasted* (Barrel Organ/Styx); *The Eye Test, Get Stuff Break Free* (National Theatre); *Everyone* (Battersea Arts Centre); *The Iphigenia Quartet* (The Gate); *Cyrano de Bergerac* (Northern Stage); *Praxis Makes Perfect* (National Theatre Wales/Berlin Festspiele); *Mad Man* (Theatre Royal Plymouth); *There has Possibly Been an Incident* (Soho Theatre/ Royal Exchange Manchester); *The Passion* (National Theatre Wales/Wildworks); *Pericles* (Regents Park).

Film and television includes: *Casualty, Doctors, The Lens, The Mysteries* (BBC); *Cycles* (Toynbee film); *The Gospel of Us* (Ffilm Cymru Wales); *Dawson's Creek Special* (Channel 4); *England My England* (Film4).

Joseph Brown | Eddie

Joseph graduated from Rose Bruford College in 2010.

Theatre credits include: *Macbeth* (National Theatre UK Tour); *Tin Soldier, The Polio Monologues* (Birds of Paradise); *Scribble* (Assemble Roxy); *Feast & Famine* (Urban Fox Theatre); *Safeword* (Traverse Theatre); *Tell Me What Giving Up Looks Like* (The Arches).

Creative Team

Tom Wentworth | Writer

Tom Wentworth is a writer for screen and theatre.

Theatre credits include: *Burke and Hare* (The Watermill/Jermyn Street Theatre/The New Wolsey Theatre); *Pen Pals* (Rural Arts); *Bully* (recipient of an MGCFutures Bursary); *No Place* (Pentabus/Paines Plough*)* and *Windy Old Fossils* (Pentabus Young Writers).

Screen credits include: *CripTales: The Real Deal, Ralph and Katie* (BBC); *Battery* (Film4). He has original projects in development with production companies including Erebus Pictures, Quay Street Productions, Silverprint Pictures and West Road Pictures.

Tom is delighted to have been commissioned to write *Little Bits of Ruined Beauty* for Pentabus after being part of the inaugural Young Writers' Programme in 2014.

Nickie Miles-Wildin | Director

Nickie Miles-Wildin, a freelance theatre and audio director who loves telling stories that are full of hope, connection, community, and challenge the structures of ordinary storytelling, reaching audiences that are sometimes excluded from theatre spaces. Nickie's work challenges the preconceptions around disability, and she aims to put those narratives centre stage through her passion in new writing and devising. Nickie was previously Joint Artistic Director and CEO of DaDa, Associate Director at Graeae where she was Head of New Writing. In 2014 Nickie co-founded TwoCan, Gloucestershire's first disabled led theatre company.

Recent theatre credits include: *Fly The Flag* (National Theatre/ Fuel); *Leave The Light On For Me* (Mind The Gap); *Kerbs* (Graeae/ Belgrade Theatre); *When This Is Over, Cuttin' It, The Tempest @ Abraham Moss* (Royal Exchange Theatre); *The Iron Man* (Graeae /Spark Arts); *The Forest of Forgotten Discos* (Contact Theatre).

Online work: *Crips Without Constraints Parts One & Two* (Graeae); *MMXX* and *ConnectFest* (Royal Exchange Theatre).

Audio: *Love Across The Ages* (BBC Radio 4/Naked Productions); *The Night Of The Living Flatpacks* (Naked Productions); *Ghost Pine* (Audible/Lamda).

Rachana Jadhav | Designer

Rachana is an award-winning theatre designer and illustrator. Rachana trained as an architect at Edinburgh College of Art and MA Scenography at Central St Martins.

Theatre, opera & dance credits include: *Total Immediate Collective Imminent Terrestrial Salvation, Menage a Trois* (National Theatre of Scotland); *Curry Tales, A Handful of Henna, Looking for Kool* (Rasa Productions); *Ghosts in the Gallery, Goldilocks, Ugly Duckling, RED* (Polka Theatre); *2020 Monologues* (Tara Arts); *Emperor's New Clothes* (Derby Theatre); *Guantanamo Boy, Her, Clocks the Greener, The Powder Monkey* (Brolly Productions).

James Mackenzie | Lighting Designer

James trained at Rose Bruford College. Recent credits include: *Unwanted Objects* (ACE Dance and Music); *Hungry Nation* (Coventry City of Culture); *Idyll* (Pentabus); *Everything But The Girl* (2Faced Dance); *Hansel and Gretel* (Uchenna Dance/ The Place); *This is an Island* (Gary Clarke/Dancexchange); *Hansel* (Salisbury Playhouse); *Run* (2Faced Dance); *Dark Wood, Deep Snow* (Northern Stage); *Ten* (Tavaziva Dance); *Jason and the Argonauts* (Courtyard Theatre); *Close Distance* (Parlor Dance); *Finding Joy* (Vamos Theatre); *Rock and Suitcase*

Story (Dance East); *The Legend of Captain Crow's Teeth* (Unicorn Theatre); *DNA* (Hull Truck); *Macbeth* (Courtyard Theatre); *Herding Cats* (Hampstead); *See* (Company Decalage); *Shattered* (Feral Productions); *Steam* (Royal Festival Hall); *Cut it Out* (Young Vic); *Speaking on Tongues* (Birmingham School of Acting). James is also the Director of the award winning ZOO Venues at the Edinburgh Festival Fringe.

Charlotte Barber | Sound Design and Composition

Charlotte Barber goes by the moniker SHAR and is a sound designer, composer, music producer and artist. She writes and produces music for theatre, film and live performance.

Theatre credits include: *Astronauts, Up The Hill, Utopia* (Royal Exchange); *Bloody Harmony* (Thickskin); *Kerbs* (Graeae); *Belle and Mary* (The Dukes); *The Accident Did Not Take Place, [insert slogan here], YESYESNONO* (Edinburgh Fringe/ UK Tours).

Film credits include: *Still Breathing* (Manchester International Festival); *House*; *Salt Stories* (Cheshire Dance).

Ben Glover | Video Design and Captions

Ben Glover is a deaf video designer and creative captioner who uses interdisciplinary skills in both creative and technical fields producing innovative and often expressive creations typically informed by his background in theatre, film and computing. He is a recent Fellow of the Royal Shakespeare Company for his research on creative captioning and a recipient of the Epic Games MegaGrants programme. He has also previously received the Mead Fellowship award for his Virtual Reality project, Simple Misunderstanding.

His recent work includes video designs for: Tubular Bells 50th Anniversary Concert Tour; *NOISE* (The Place); *Saturn Returns* (Southbank Centre); *The Lesson* (Southwark Playhouse); *The Paradis Files* (Tour); *RED* (Polka Theatre); *Different Owners at Sunrise* (Roundhouse Studio); *Americana!* (Hellenic Centre); Coventry City of Culture, Liverpool Arab Arts Festival, Pukkelpop and Burning Man Festival.

Stephanie Dale | Dramaturg

Stephanie's current commissions include: *Spinning the Moon* (Dorchester Community Plays Association); *Salt* (Poole Lighthouse/Angel Exit).

Theatre credits include: *Persuasion* (Theatre 6, London/National tour); *Alice in Wonderland* (Theatre in the Quarter); *Moonfleet* (Bristol Old

Vic Theatre School/South West Tour); *The Chester Mystery Plays* (Chester); *The Witches' Promise* (Birmingham REP).

Radio includes: *Losing Paradise, What is Missing from Your Life?, Believe Me* (Nominated for the Tinniswood Award) (BBC Radio 4).

Natalie Grady | Voice & Accent Coach

Theatre credits include: *The Glass Menagerie, Nora, Glee and Me, Wuthering Heights, Gypsy, Light Falls, West Side Story, Queens of the Coal Age* (Royal Exchange); *Hangmen* (Golden Theatre Broadway); *Kes, The Last Yankee, A View From the Bridge, Two, Two 2* (Octagon Theatre); *Tom's Midnight Garden, The Beauty Queen of Leenane* (Theatre by the Lake); *Celebrated Virgins* (Theatre Clwyd); *Hull and High Water, A Short History of Tractors in Ukrainian, The Last Testament of Lillian Bilocca* (Hull Truck); *The Nico Project* (MIF); *Scoring a Century* (British Youth Opera); *Lancastrians* (Junction 8); *Jess and Joe Forever* (Stephen Joseph Theatre); *Chicken Soup* (Sheffield Crucible); *Bread and Roses, Jumpers for Goalposts, Brassed Off* (Oldham Coliseum); *Little Women, Beggars Opera, Little Shop of Horrors, Blue Stockings, Wizard of Oz* (Storyhouse); *Hoard Festival, Seeing the Lights, Beryl* (New Vic Theatre); *La Vie Parisienne, Street Scene* (RNCM); *To Kill a Mockingbird* (UK tour/Barbican).

TV and Film credits include: *One Day* (Netflix); *Better, Happy Valley, The Reckoning, The Gallows Pole, Rules of the Game, Time* (BBC); *Ackley Bridge, The Cure, Somewhere Boy, Trip* (C4); *Red Rose* (BBC/Netflix); *Anne, Mcdonald and Dodds, Stephen, The Ipcress File* (ITV); *Jingle Bell Christmas* (Hallmark); *Wolfe* (Sky); *All Creatures Great And Small* (C5 and PBS for the US); *Gwen* (Endor productions); *Your Christmas Or Mine.*

Lizzie Wiggs | Movement

Recent movement director credits include: *Chang, Eng and Me (and Me)* (Wattle and Daub Figure Theatre); *My Mother Said I Never Should* (Theatre by the Lake).

Recent theatre credits include: *The Kitchen Circus Project* (Cirque Bijou); *Constellations* (Ad Infinitum); *Hidden Voices* (Strike a Light/GL4 Festival); *They Only Come at Night: Resurrection, Mapping the City, Converging paths, 59 Minutes to Save Christmas* (Slung Low); *The Black Diamond, The Marat/Sade* (Punchdrunk); *The Whale* (Circo Rum Ba Ba); *Commissioners* (Boundless Theatre); *The Unholy Trinity, The Revenge of Mr Trout, The Mischief Before Christmas* (State of Play Theatre); *The Dinner Table, The Birthday Party* (Wet Picnic).

Lizzie is currently an Associate Director for the National Theatre Connections Festival.

PENTABUS

'Pentabus is probably one of the most important theatre companies in the country, where it has led, other new writing theatres – such as the Royal Court – have followed' The Telegraph

Pentabus is the nation's rural theatre company. We are the only professional theatre company in the UK whose vision is singularly rural. We tour new plays about the contemporary rural world to new audiences in village halls, fields, festivals and theatres, telling stories with local relevance, plus national and international impact.

We believe that every person living in an isolated rural community has a right to exceptional theatre. We are based in a Victorian school in rural Shropshire, and to date all of our work has been made here. It then tours village halls and theatres locally and nationally. Over four and a half decades we've produced 175 new plays, reached over half a million audience members, won a prestigious South Bank Show award, a Fringe First and were the first to live stream from a village hall. We have hosted a writer in residence since 2014 and they have gone on to be commissioned by the Birmingham Rep, the Bush, HighTide, Nottingham Playhouse, the National Theatre, Royal Court and Royal Welsh College.

We are a champion for rural young people aged 16 to 30 and Pentabus Young Company is our programme offering workshops, masterclasses, work experience and mentorships, as well as the opportunity to join our Young Writers' Group, which has been running for nine years. Previous participants of the Young Writers' Group have had their work presented at Ludlow Fringe, Latitude Festival and Hereford Courtyard. It is a springboard into further study and the arts industry.

You can find out more about us at **pentabus.co.uk**

Twitter: @pentabustheatre | Facebook: @pentabustheatre
Instagram: @Pentabustheatrecompany

Pentabus Theatre Company, Bromfield, Ludlow, Shropshire, SY8 2JU

Pentabus is a registered charity (Number 287909). We rely on the generosity of our donors, small and large, to help us to continue to make world-class theatre. We would like to thank all our supporters including:

Torchbearers

Madeleine Bedford, Richard Burbidge, Camilla Harrison, Diane Lennan, Camilla Harrison, Alison McLean, Joseph Motley, Sophie Motley, Michael Penn, Ros Robins, Hermione Salwey, Annabel Stacey, Neil Stuttard, Barbara Ann Tweedie

Ragleth/Beacons

Cecilia Motley

Wrekin

James Mayor

Pentabus' Business Supporters

BRITPART

Pentabus is also supported by the Adlard Family Charitable Foundation, the Clive Richards Foundation, the Elmley Foundation, the Hall Garth Trust, the Haystack Trust, Herefordshire Community Foundation, the Millichope Foundation, Pilotlight & the Weston Charity Awards.

UNLIMITED...

Unlimited is an arts commissioning body that supports, funds and promotes new work by disabled artists for UK and international audiences. Our mission is to commission extraordinary work from disabled artists that will change and challenge the world. Funded by Arts Council England, Creative Scotland, Arts Council of Wales, Paul Hamlyn Foundation and British Council, since 2013, Unlimited has supported over 460 artists with over £4.9 million reaching audiences of over 5 million making it the largest supporter of disabled artists world-wide.

Connect with us

weareunlimited.org.uk

Twitter: @weareunltd | Facebook: @weareunltd | Instagram: @weareunltd

LITTLE BITS OF RUINED BEAUTY

Tom Wentworth

Acknowledgements

With enormous thanks to: Nickie Miles-Wildin for her
continued belief in the play and brilliant direction; Stephanie
Dale, dramaturg (and therapist!); Maeve Bolger, agent
extraordinaire; Elle While, Amber Knipe and all staff at
Pentabus past and present; Ellie Liddell-Crewe, Jo Verrent and
everyone at Unlimited; Stewart Pringle and everyone at the
National Theatre New Work Department; Chloe Todd-Fordham
and Jenny Sealey and everyone at Graeae for commissioning
the original play; all the actors who have read and informed
the play at various stages – Amanda Root, Tina Gray, Philippa
Cole, Joseph Alessi and Adam Fenton, but special thanks to the
cast of this production: Nigel Barrett and Joseph Brown who
have brought so much joy, humour and talent to the rehearsal
room, as well as the brilliant backstage crew and creative team
who have brought the production so splendidly to life. To all my
friends and family who have supported me during the writing
process, especially The Defectors (you know who you are!);
Steph Morris for endless proofreading and patience, and, finally,
everyone at Nick Hern Books for publishing this edition.

Characters

TERRY, *a father, early sixties*
EDDIE, *a son, mid-twenties*

This text went to press before the end of rehearsals and so may differ slightly from the play as performed.

Note on the Text

A slash (/) indicates overlapping dialogue.

An ellipsis (...) indicates a character hasn't finished their train of thought.

A dash (–) indicates an interruption.

Words in [brackets] should not be spoken.

Lynham should be pronounced 'Line-am'.

The set is physically eroding as father and son slowly unpick the cause of all their pain.

In each scene the boxes contain different items which signify the time of year.

As the play progresses, Wenlock Edge slowly begins to creep into the flat, so we are still definitely in the flat but yet also in amongst the trees...

The play is set in Bridgnorth in 2022 but Shropshire, as A. E. Housman wrote of it in a letter, is 'not exactly a real place'. Instead, it is a mix of myth, remembered and the real place.

When he's stressed, Terry paces, until he later can't, while Eddie is constantly on his phone.

The acts of care, etc. should be reimagined to suit the specific impairments of the actors.

The character of Eddie must always be played by an actor who identifies as disabled.

While this production chooses to include Christopher Logue's beautiful poem 'Come to the Edge', if the cost of including this proves prohibitive to a production, the play may be performed without – simply omit the poem and observe the final stage direction.

A flat behind a corner shop. Not run-down but certainly lived in.

1.

May. The flat is being used as an overflow storage room. The whole space is filled with boxes which contain Easter eggs and cute chick tat, etc.

EDDIE. Sorry. I didn't have any cash.

TERRY. I suppose cash is too good for you in London?

EDDIE. I'll pay you back.

TERRY. If you'd have given me some warning, Edward, I'd have picked you up.

EDDIE. It's Eddie. You know I'm Eddie. (*Beat.*) It was a last-minute decision.

TERRY. All I'm saying is it would have saved me the expense of a taxi.

You've put weight on.

EDDIE. It's muscle.

TERRY. Then you and that muscle can make yourselves useful. (*Of boxes.*) Chuck these in your old bedroom.

EDDIE. You're putting chocolate bunnies in my bedroom?

EDDIE *shifts a large box into the other room.*

TERRY. No. I'm putting chocolate bunnies in my bedroom. I sleep in your old room these days. I've run out of space in the shop.

EDDIE (*emerging again*). That room's already jam-packed. That whole room is Easter eggs.

TERRY. I order in bulk. (*Beat.*) One box too much for you, was it?

They both shift boxes. EDDIE finds it hard but is still speedy. He can't help noticing his dad is a little out of breath – yet hiding it well.

Surprised you remembered what address to give the taxi driver. You're either out of choices or out of luck.

EDDIE. It's been –

TERRY. Five years.

EDDIE. – Hard.

TERRY. I've nothing in. I expect you've still got an appetite.

EDDIE. Any chance of a chocolate bunny?

TERRY. You want to work your way through my profits?

EDDIE. Not even an ear?! (*Beat.*) You'd have let Mum.

TERRY. I let her get away with a lot of things. I had actually just heated up a lasagne. Only a ping meal but... Fancy half?

He dashes off into the kitchen. EDDIE looks around. He can't really believe he's back. TERRY returns with two plates of congealing lasagne.

What do you say to that?

EDDIE. What do you say to fish and chips?

TERRY. Fish and chips will play havoc with my acid reflux.

TERRY eats, EDDIE pushes his around the plate.

So, that university of yours given you the sack?

EDDIE. No! Why would you think that?

TERRY. It's got to be something dramatic.

EDDIE. I phoned.

TERRY. At Christmas.

EDDIE. I left voicemails. Phones work two ways, you know. You can call back.

TERRY. You're always out. Anyway, the shop's non-stop. How was the train?

EDDIE. Packed, as usual, couldn't get a seat. The driver rang Telford from the train but of course there was no assistance waiting. I had to ask a stranger to help me get down.

TERRY. Emily Parsons got her case nicked when she went to Exeter. Great Western claimed it was an accident... I wrote to them for her but – [no good.]

EDDIE. Kind of you.

TERRY. You do what you can. Come on then, what trouble are you in?

EDDIE. Dad. It's not like that.

TERRY. Whatever you've done.

EDDIE. Dad. Really.

TERRY. We both know you can be hot-headed. Prone to your little tantrums.

EDDIE. When I was a teenager.

TERRY. Tell me and I'll sort it. Remember those boys down The Grove?

EDDIE. I can look after myself.

TERRY. You leave it to me. I know people.

EDDIE. Oh yeah, you know everyone. Good old Terry Lynham.

TERRY. I can look after myself.

EDDIE. I'm not in trouble. I'm writing a book.

Silence. EDDIE *wants a reaction from his dad. It's a beat too long.*

And that's exactly why I don't tell you things.

TERRY. It's great. Really.

EDDIE. The university have given me a sabbatical from teaching.

TERRY. A sabbatical? That's… amazing, son.

EDDIE. Didn't think they were going to let me but –

TERRY. I got back into reading during lockdown.

EDDIE. Yeah?

TERRY. Spy thrillers. Tom Bradby. Undercover stuff. Is yours going to be like that?

EDDIE. It's non-fiction.

TERRY. Historical? I like a good Tudor romp.

EDDIE. There'll definitely be some history in it, yeah.

TERRY. So?

EDDIE. It's just a kind of academic thing.

TERRY. Go on then. Scared I won't get it?

EDDIE. This is just a working title at the moment. I mean I'm not reinventing the wheel / or anything.

TERRY. For god's sake, Edward, just tell me.

EDDIE. *How Self-Care and Connection Can Save the Planet – Mental and Global Wellness, Disability, Climate Change and Social Responsibility.* (*Pause.*) I'll clear away.

TERRY. Leave it. Is it because you're…

EDDIE. Disabled?

TERRY. Is it because of that they're paying you to write this thing.

EDDIE. It's a book. And no, it's not. Thing is I can't really write at home. Paper-thin walls.

TERRY. That's London for you.

EDDIE. I'm sure I'll write a lot better here, with the quiet and everything. Plus, the book's meant to be about isolation, connection, social responsibility, I could use you as a case study.

TERRY. So, it's not enough eating me out of house and home…

EDDIE. Just for a month.

TERRY's face says it all.

Maybe less. It's not like we're going to be together all the time, is it?

They both laugh nervously.

After all, nobody wants that, do they?

TERRY. No.

EDDIE. I get it's all a bit zero to eleven but – I did genuinely want to see you.

TERRY. Nice to have a bit of help... In the shop.

EDDIE. I thought you said –

TERRY. Family's different. 'Lynham and Son' the sign says.

EDDIE. Dad.

TERRY. One shift a day. Help me get on top of the admin.

EDDIE. It kind of defeats the point. If I'm trying to write.

TERRY. Three hours a day.

EDDIE. Two point five.

TERRY. Plenty of trains back to London.

EDDIE. Alright. Three.

TERRY. Pleasure doing business with you.

EDDIE (*rubs his leg*). Ow. Cramp.

TERRY. You still doing your physio?

EDDIE. Let it all slide a bit to be honest.

TERRY. You shouldn't.

EDDIE. Have you any idea how difficult it was during lockdown? Zoom physio? It just doesn't work, Dad.

Beat.

TERRY. What do you say to a pint down The Shakespeare?

EDDIE. You're going to have to hold onto me going down the hill.

TERRY. You'll be holding onto me.

EDDIE. Sure.

> EDDIE *gets his coat. They go through the palaver of putting it on again.* EDDIE *bats his dad away but* TERRY *is determined to 'help'.*

TERRY. Come on, you're buying!

> *They go.*

...

TERRY *stands, alone and silent in the calm and the trees of Wenlock Edge. (It should feel a long way from the shop and the flat at this point.)*

TERRY*'s feet are firmly planted, his eyes skywards, looking out at the view.*

If you didn't know better, you'd think he was praying...

2.

Two weeks later.

The room is a complete mess. The room has now become EDDIE*'s living space.*

Rain hammers outside.

TERRY*'s walking boots are by the door. He enters and slumps into a chair.*

EDDIE *rushes in – knackered and wet through. He tries to take off his damp clothes but they cling. It's hard. He struggles with them.*

TERRY (*under his breath*). Total pigsty. (*To* EDDIE.) Eddie is that you?

EDDIE. Who else would it be?

TERRY. You went out? In this?

EDDIE*'s head is now stuck inside his polo shirt.*

EDDIE *is becoming more and more frustrated.*

EDDIE *is desperately trying to get free.* EDDIE *finally gets free.*

I needed some fresh air.

TERRY. You're soaked.

EDDIE. I didn't know it was going to bucket down.

TERRY. Should have asked me. I do the weather round here. Famous for it. Showers now, thunder later.

EDDIE. Thank you, Shefali.

TERRY. Thank my seaweed. Picked that up on Cromer Beach when you were seven.

EDDIE. Six.

TERRY. Seven.

EDDIE. Six. My ice cream got pinched by a seagull. After one of those horrific long hikes Mum made us go on.

TERRY. You fell backwards into a rock pool. Had to bring you home in a black bin liner. You sulked all the way back.

EDDIE. Wouldn't you?

TERRY. Right. I've got to get over to Mrs Henderson's.

EDDIE. You can't cut her grass in this.

TERRY. She'll find me something else to do.

EDDIE. I bet she will. In the last week you've taken her cat to the vet, tested her smoke alarm, and you mended a lamp for her place in Wales.

TERRY. Nothing wrong with helping out a neighbour.

EDDIE. Bet she doesn't ask any of her other neighbours?

TERRY. They're not all as fit as me. Besides, we can't all sit around 'thinking'.

Pause. TERRY *realises he's overstepped the mark.* EDDIE *starts wrestling his damp trousers off.*

Eddie. Son. Come on. Let me help.

EDDIE. No. Thanks.

TERRY. It'd be much quicker.

EDDIE. No thanks. Not like I've anything to do. I'm only 'thinking'.

TERRY *heads out.* EDDIE *continues to struggle. Finally, defeated, he gives up.*

Meanwhile, TERRY *keeps popping in and out looking for car keys, aftershave, etc. He's relishing waiting for the inevitable.*

Dad.

TERRY *appears round the door. Smiles.* EDDIE *swallows, clutches his neck – can't quite bring himself to ask.*

TERRY (*relishing this*). You rang?

TERRY *helps him out of the wet clothes and into dry ones.*

EDDIE. Don't be so rough. You'll have the hairs on my legs out!

TERRY. Stop being so soft.

EDDIE. I inherited hairy legs from you.

TERRY. Nothing wrong with my legs. Other leg.

They finish.

EDDIE. Cheers. I won't wait up.

TERRY. It's not like that. Marina isn't –

EDDIE. Oh, Marina, is it?

TERRY (*running away*). See you later.

EDDIE. I suppose there's no chance of you – ? Your old bed. You did say you would. Only this sofa bed's quite... lumpy.

TERRY. I'll get to it.

EDDIE. When?

TERRY. Nothing stopping you making a start, is there?

EDDIE. 'Spose not.

TERRY. There you go then.

EDDIE. I went in there yesterday.

TERRY. I gotta go.

EDDIE. It still smells of her behind that lot. All her lotions and potions on the dressing table.

TERRY. Have you seen my ear defenders? I put them down and now I can't find them. (*Heading for the door.*) I swear someone comes in at night / and shifts stuff.

EDDIE. I don't know what to do about it, Dad.

TERRY. See you later.

EDDIE. Dad?

TERRY. Marina's garden is on such a slope it's like mowing Wenlock Edge. Your mum loved it up there. Blakeway Coppice, Major's Leap... Her escape.

Beat.

EDDIE. Dad. Earlier. I knew it was raining. I can't explain but I had to see other people. Had to go somewhere. Until I remembered there's actually nowhere for me to go. I just walked along the rugby pitch and thought... there's nobody left.

TERRY. Darren Scholes came into the shop. He was asking after you.

EDDIE. Darren! God, I haven't seen him in...? Mum always reckoned he'd go far.

TERRY. Prison. He's just got out.

Beat.

EDDIE. Here I am, meant to be writing about 'self-care' and it's like I threw my independence into the bottom of the river.

TERRY. Working in the shop is how I meet people. You want to hear some good stories? Juicy gossip. Apparently Ronnie Smethwaite's wife has changed all the locks and was seen doing a solo tango totally starkers on their front lawn.

EDDIE. I've lost my care. My benefits.

TERRY. When? What are you talking about?

EDDIE. They've moved me from Disability Living Allowance to Personal Independence Payment.

TERRY. Independence sounds good.

EDDIE. You'd think. It's meant to pay for my care, my needs.

TERRY. Don't tell me, they've moved the goalposts.

EDDIE. Yep, they've stopped my payments. I got myself into a bit of hot water.

TERRY. There's no money. Not until I'm dead and buried.

EDDIE. Don't think I want to be relying on you.

TERRY. But here you are. I don't understand how you could get yourself in such a mess. I wouldn't do that with road tax.

EDDIE. We're not talking about road tax.

TERRY. Your mum was the carer. She did all the forms.

EDDIE. Right. (*Beat.*) All she wanted was for you to be at home. With us. The three of us together.

TERRY. I wanted you to be at her funeral. We can't always have everything we want.

The air is heavy.

After a pause, EDDIE *flops onto the sofa and puts his headphones on.*

...

TERRY *runs on Wenlock Edge – he is not exactly unfit. However, he is taking his training seriously. He finally stops, out of breath. Suddenly, it's as if he sees himself for the first time – what is he doing?! He laughs at the sky.*

Meanwhile, EDDIE *looks at drone images of Wenlock Edge on his laptop...*

3.

June. Night.

The bedroom is still not cleared. The living room is silent. Commotion outside.

A frustrated TERRY *enters with a very drunk* EDDIE. *He's continually almost falling over. (Perhaps we notice that this is more physically stressful to* TERRY *than he is letting on.)*

TERRY. Let's get you in, / shall we?

EDDIE. You're never going to do it.

TERRY. Bed.

EDDIE. Not bed. Want another drink.

TERRY. Bed. Edward.

EDDIE. You'll never walk two-hundred miles.

TERRY. What? Nobody's walking two-hundred miles.

EDDIE. I want another drink.

TERRY. Water.

EDDIE. Poison.

TERRY. Water. Or nothing.

EDDIE. Nothing.

TERRY. Stay there. (*He goes and quickly returns with a pint glass.*)

EDDIE. You like the outside, don't you?

TERRY. I like sleep more.

EDDIE. Mum said you were born grumpy.

TERRY. Practical. Bedtime.

EDDIE. I always wanted to cheer you up, but she would just say, 'Dad's a grump – '

TERRY. Edward.

EDDIE. That's why she went walking on Wenlock Edge so much.

TERRY. Seriously.

EDDIE *swings his arms dramatically, accidentally opening* TERRY*'s coat – revealing pyjamas underneath.*

EDDIE. Ha! You're already ready for bed.

TERRY. I was in bed. Who comes to the rescue when you're in London?

EDDIE. I have friends. Thousands.

TERRY. Facebook doesn't count.

EDDIE. I had Amy. I had a girlfriend. But, I don't need rescuing. I am an adult... a fully adult person.

TERRY. Looks like it.

He's got him onto the bed now.

Drink up.

EDDIE. Cheers! (*The water spills*.) I've wet the bed.

TERRY *turns to go*.

You can't leave me like this.

TERRY. It'll dry. Go to sleep.

EDDIE. That's cruel. Why are you being so cruel?!

TERRY. I'm going training in the morning.

EDDIE. Yeah, yeah, yeah.

TERRY. When are you going to grow up?

TERRY *switches the light off*.

EDDIE. I don't like the dark...

TERRY. Sleep.

EDDIE. Mum would never leave me.

TERRY *snaps the light on. He looks at his pathetic son*.

He helps EDDIE *onto a chair*.

Sorry Dad.

TERRY. No you're not.

TERRY *has the sheets off the bed*.

EDDIE. You never really liked me.

TERRY. Don't push it.

EDDIE. You never wanted a 'handicapped' son... You wanted a son who would live up to your ridiculous sign.

EDDIE *tugs at the sheet, hard. It almost rips, he almost topples*. TERRY *gets it*.

TERRY. Why do you do this? Why do you always do this? It was the same when you were a teenager.

EDDIE. Just a few drinks and some pool at The Crown.

TERRY. It's never a few drinks, though, is it?

EDDIE. Just letting off steam.

TERRY. I really hoped we were done with all this. Being dragged out in the middle of the night. The emergencies. Police cells. Coming to get you from God knows where, in God knows what state. You never did know the meaning of the word responsibility, did you?

EDDIE. I am responsible.

TERRY. Act like it.

EDDIE. I got you this. (*He produces a crumpled card from his jacket pocket.*) Happy Father's Day. Sorry. It got a bit... mangled.

TERRY. Not the only one.

He starts going at the sheet again.

EDDIE. It was just a few drinks. With Darren.

TERRY. Darren?

EDDIE. Yeah. He's changed. Really got himself together. Got a job and a flat, and –

TERRY. A criminal record.

EDDIE. You should give him a chance. He's decent. He's finding life on the outside... [tricky] Why do people have to be so small-minded?

EDDIE drinks the water down. EDDIE suddenly seems very sober.

I can do this.

TERRY. No. This sheet and I. We've come this far.

The sheet's on. TERRY has got hold of the duvet now.

EDDIE. Dad, I'm quite capable.

TERRY. I like to do a job properly.

EDDIE. Darren says you're doing the Bridgnorth Walk next year.

TERRY. Yes? And?

EDDIE. Everyone likes a comedy entry.

EDDIE takes the duvet off him.

TERRY. It's for charity. Macmillan Nurses.

EDDIE. When it came back again…

TERRY hands EDDIE two corners of the duvet.

TERRY. They were good to her.

EDDIE. You should have told me.

The bed is made.

TERRY helps EDDIE in and tucks him up.

TERRY. Come with me to Wenlock Edge.

EDDIE. I can't.

TERRY's on his way out. He turns out the light.

…

Daytime.

TERRY runs along Wenlock Edge, training. He spots there's no one around. He stops. He's out of breath but doesn't want to show it. He holds his back – a twinge.

He sits on the ground. He takes a letter out of his pocket. Pauses. Will he open it?

He breathes hard. Quickly opens the letter and pulls it out.

As he reads, his face falls. He's tempted to tear the letter up but resists.

Instead, he folds the letter and puts it back in his pocket. Then he runs on.

4.

A couple of weeks later.

EDDIE *is trying to write. He hammers the laptop keys.*

Deletes. Puts his head in his hands.

Distracted, he keeps looking over at the bedroom door. He shifts himself on the sofa bed. He can't get comfortable.

No. He must work. He tries to get back to what he is writing but he can't.

Eventually he gives in. He has to clear that room.

He ventures in and drags a heavy box full of stuff to the middle of the floor, with proper effort. Again, with effort, he gets himself onto the floor.

He rummages through letters, papers and photographs, throwing the occasional item straight into the bin. Eventually, he discovers a large shoebox. He holds it for a moment, afraid to open it.

Deep breath. He whips off the lid. He laughs.

It's full of Dinky cars. He tips them onto the floor: two fire engines, a Jaguar police car, a Ford Cortina. Each one is battered and loved.

He immediately starts whizzing them round the carpet.

TERRY *enters with beers. His eyes immediately light up.*

TERRY. My Dinkys!

EDDIE. You gave them to me.

TERRY. Let's call it a long-term loan. Where did you find them? (*Handing him a beer.*) Cheers.

EDDIE. Cheers.

TERRY. Budge up.

TERRY*'s on the floor now with the police car.*

Oh no! What's that? An emergency on top of Clee Hill?
Don't worry, madam, the police are on their way!

EDDIE. Oi! I was always the police car.

TERRY. Sorry, son. I'm driving. You can navigate.

EDDIE. Hey. You were always the fire engine.

TERRY. There's no time to even finish my pint.

EDDIE. The police shouldn't drink and drive. (*He tries to take control.*)

TERRY (*making the white noise of a police radio*). Many dead... Suspected house fire in Severn Street...

EDDIE (*excited*). House fire?! You'll be wanting the – fire engine!

EDDIE *whizzes the fire engine round the carpet. They both play, making siren noises. They're like kids totally absorbed in the game, the happiest we've ever seen them.*

They continue to play. After a while...

TERRY. I'll book the Dilraz.

EDDIE. You can never have too much curry.

TERRY. We don't have to...

EDDIE. I'd like to.

TERRY. Yeah, but we don't have to go yet.

EDDIE. Plenty of time.

TERRY. Now, my turn with the fire engine!

EDDIE (*pouring more beers*). And here's to more drinking on duty!

They clink glasses – cheers.

TERRY *practically collapses on the sofa bed – it's really uncomfortable.*

TERRY. Ow. I never realised this bed was so... You can feel every spring.

EDDIE. It needs to go, Dad. If I have to sleep on those rusty springs once more – Plus, I'm not used to sleeping in a single bed.

TERRY. Get used to it.

EDDIE. I don't miss Amy's night-time activities.

TERRY. Oh yeah?

EDDIE. She's the only person I know who can talk and snore at the same time.

TERRY. With a talent like that I'm sorry I didn't get to meet her. Why did you never introduce us?

EDDIE. Amy doesn't 'do' outside of the M25.

A shared look between them.

TERRY (*he starts to pack the bed away*). This bed's been good to our family. A real friend to those in need.

EDDIE. Okay. But I'm clearing that room, if it kills me.

With the bed now away, TERRY *starts getting more cars out, building a bridge, infrastructure, etc. He's going to town.*

TERRY. I was sure we'd thrown all these out.

EDDIE. My cars? / No way!

TERRY. Grandad gave them to me.

EDDIE. They were under a load of junk.

TERRY. What happened to your Eddie Stobart truck?

EDDIE. Dunno.

TERRY. Great tenth birthday present that.

EDDIE. Yeah. For me or for you?

TERRY goes to the box.

TERRY. Must be knocking about somewhere...

He begins rummaging, casually.

EDDIE. What happened to my Meccano set?

TERRY. Bin. It was broken.

EDDIE. We never did finish that Ferris wheel...

> EDDIE *hasn't noticed* TERRY *has stopped; his smile gone. He's frozen. He's found an angel with a crooked halo.*

You lost half the pieces up the Hoover anyway...

TERRY. She always let you decorate the tree.

EDDIE. Dad?

> TERRY *stands with it in his hands. Still frozen.*

TERRY. She made it the year you were born.

EDDIE. Old pipe cleaners and bits of tinsel. Nice one, Mum.

> TERRY *lets it drop back into the box. He can't bear to hold the angel, it's too much.*

TERRY. I'll get changed. Clean shirts, if we're going out.

> TERRY *goes, silent and deliberate.*

> EDDIE *looks at the box. Should he continue?*

> *It's compulsive. He can't stop.*

> *He pulls out another box of random junk.*

> *He pulls out the angel. He tries to straighten her halo but it refuses to remain in place. He strokes her. He finds baubles and some tinsel.*

> *What should he do with the angel?*

> *A beat before he gently places her on the mantelpiece.*

> *He finds* TERRY*'s letter.* EDDIE*'s eyes widen as he reads. He stuffs it in his pocket, as* TERRY *enters in a clean shirt.*

I can't wait for my korma.

EDDIE. What? No vindaloo? Not going soft in your old age, are you, Dad?

TERRY. Acid reflux. (*Beat.*) Look at all this mess, Edward.

EDDIE. I'll sort it.

TERRY *immediately starts clearing the cars away.* EDDIE *is still sorting photos.*

Don't put them away. I don't know half these people. Mum loved a duplicate, didn't she? Look, here's all the kids she helped with their reading.

TERRY. You were so embarrassed she was in your class you refused to acknowledge her existence. She only volunteered in the first place to keep an eye on you.

EDDIE. Oh my god, there's Darren. Those glasses! And there's me. My spots. (*He bins the photo.*)

TERRY (*getting his coat*)....And I'll get some naan. Peshwari maybe. I like to go a bit exotic from time to time.

EDDIE. I reckon Mum kept photos of every local group she was ever part of. She always made me go with her – choir, book group, art classes. Any chance she got to socialise.

TERRY. She always wanted you to integrate. Or to get away from this place.

EDDIE (*holding up a handmade thank-you card*). And she loved a lost cause. 'Dear Sally, Just to say thank you for giving me a bed for the night...' Look, Dad – who was this?

TERRY *takes it, but can't look. It cuts deep. He's desperate to get out.*

TERRY. Don't know.

EDDIE (*picking up another photo*). Dad? Where was this? I look about twelve. Must have been the summer before she first got ill. Mum, you and me in a giant teacup. Can you remember?

TERRY (*without looking*). No.

TERRY *is almost out the door, his eyes fixed on escape. He is frozen.*

EDDIE. Why am I eating in every photo? And what about this one? Looks like we're on one of her famous hikes looking at the fossils of Wenlock Edge. You and I look a lot happier than I bet we felt. I guess she'd bribed me with a big mug of hot chocolate at the end. (*Beat.*) What are we going to do with all this stuff?

TERRY (*turning to face* EDDIE. *He looks much older than he did earlier*). It took her quickly in the end. All those months of clock watching then –

EDDIE. Dad.

TERRY. She was standing at the sink; bit of indigestion. Potato peeler in her hand. All those months of pain, just to have a heart attack. Like switching off a lightbulb, they said. But what do they know?

EDDIE. If you'd told me –

TERRY. It's done.

EDDIE. I would have come back.

TERRY (*would you?*). It's over...

EDDIE. And all this?

TERRY (*shrugs*). Chuck it. I don't care.

EDDIE. But these things. They're her.

TERRY. Are we going or what?

EDDIE *exits.*

TERRY *looks round. He spots the angel, tries to correct her halo. No good. He puts her delicately back on the mantelpiece behind a photo of a recently arrived litter of puppies and a postcard from Barmouth.*

He goes.

...

TERRY *is on Wenlock Edge as the light fades. He kneels on the ground, his head in his hands.*

He lies flat on the earth.

It is all too much. He cries.

5.

August.

The bedroom is now cleared and a habitable living space, though two overflowing boxes of stuff still sit accusingly in the corner, eyeing them both. (The angel is still on the mantelpiece.)

EDDIE *is writing when* TERRY *starts putting his running shoes on. (Moving is harder than when we last saw him.)*

EDDIE*'s phone beeps. He reads the text and puts his phone down, despondent.* TERRY *notices he's bored.*

What's the date?

TERRY (*checks watch*). Eighteenth of August. When was the last time you went out?

EDDIE. I'm sure there was something this week?

TERRY. You should get some sun on your face.

EDDIE. I've been trying to organise a class reunion.

TERRY. Nice idea.

EDDIE. Yeah, just some of the old gang. But everyone's either got new babies or new puppies. Or both. (*Beat.*) You're going training again?

TERRY. Want to crack my PB.

EDDIE. It's a walk, Dad. For charity.

TERRY. Can't let my sponsors down.

EDDIE. With ten months to go? You are so competitive.

TERRY. I am not competitive. I'm proactive.

EDDIE. Dare I mention the parents' sack race?

TERRY. I was robbed. And I'm totally over it.

He starts comically running on the spot.

I'll be off then.

EDDIE. And exactly how much of your training is having tea and chat at Mrs Henderson's?

TERRY. I take my training seriously.

EDDIE. Dunk the biscuit, lift the biscuit, dunk the biscuit, lift the biscuit...

TERRY. She's in Barmouth this week, if you must know. She asked me again. But this place won't run itself. Don't forget, it's your turn to cook.

EDDIE. I'll make a big salad, or something.

TERRY (*starts heading out*). Anything. As long as it's got chips with it. (*Beat.*) Have you seen my sunscreen?

EDDIE. By my bed.

TERRY. Oh. That's okay.

TERRY *looks towards the door.*

I'll manage without. Better catch the sun while I can. They had hail in Cleobury North earlier. Big stones.

Nervously, EDDIE gets a letter out of his pocket. Is this the right moment?

(*Setting off at speed.*) Gotta run, as they say.

EDDIE *unfolds the letter.*

EDDIE. 'Dear Mr Lynham, I am writing to inform you of your appointment at the / Royal Shrewsbury –'

TERRY *stops. His eyes widen. His face white.*

TERRY. You shouldn't read / people's private correspondence.

EDDIE. '...Hospital on the seventeenth.' Yesterday.

TERRY. Give that here.

Reluctantly EDDIE *passes it over.* TERRY *throws it in the bin.*

EDDIE. I would have come with you.

TERRY. It's nothing to do / with you.

EDDIE. It is. Of course / it is.

TERRY. Whatever your generation thinks it doesn't help to 'talk' / all the time. It's private. That's all.

EDDIE. If it was me you'd want to know. Wouldn't you?

TERRY. That's different.

EDDIE. No it isn't.

TERRY. It's private. That's all.

TERRY starts pacing. He simply can't keep still.

EDDIE. Why do I still expect you to change? When all the evidence says you just aren't capable. And... and why the hell do I care so much?

TERRY just shrugs.

How long have you known?

TERRY. Just leave it.

He attempts to set off but there's a twinge. He instinctively holds his back.

EDDIE (*of back*). How long?

TERRY. Six months. (*Off* EDDIE's *look of surprise.*) Or so.

EDDIE. All this time.

TERRY. A bit longer. Maybe.

EDDIE. You can't do this again. Not this time.

TERRY. It's not the same.

EDDIE. I had a right to be told.

TERRY. I got hold of you as soon as I could. Anyway, this is different.

EDDIE. How? I'm right here, Dad. Right. Here.

TERRY. It's osteoarthritis. Early onset.

EDDIE. That's bones and joints / and –

TERRY. It's nothing. They're probably wrong.

EDDIE. Oh yeah, highly trained doctors… bound to be wrong.

TERRY. Just one of those things.

EDDIE. A cold is 'one of those things'.

TERRY. I'm just not as fast as I used to be. Not as fit.

EDDIE. You didn't need a doctor to tell you that.

TERRY. My discs are crumbling. They said I need to keep moving.

EDDIE. So, all this… (*Indicating his trainers.*) The walk… unbelievable. There must be stuff they can do? Treatment?

TERRY. Edward. This isn't your fight.

EDDIE. So, you are going to fight it, yes?

TERRY. I'm going to keep going / like I've always done.

EDDIE. You're going to kick it so hard –

TERRY. I couldn't kick anything at the moment.

EDDIE. – it won't know what's hit it!

TERRY. Just let me do things my own way.

EDDIE. Why didn't you tell me?

TERRY. Because I knew we'd have all this…

EDDIE. All what?

TERRY. This. This. These hysterics.

EDDIE. You're the only person who ever / thought –

TERRY. You were the same when you were a child. I didn't tell
you because I didn't want you to be upset.

Exasperated, EDDIE *heads over to the boxes and begins
sorting his mum's stuff, loudly.*

EDDIE. No, Dad. You never told me, because I never entered
your head.

TERRY. That's not true.

EDDIE. Once I was out that door you forgot I existed. Just like
last time.

TERRY. How many times do we have to go / through this?

EDDIE. Mum was the one who phoned –

TERRY. What if I'd nothing to say? (*Lighter.*) You know me,
I'm a bugger.

EDDIE. – until one day the phone stopped ringing.

TERRY. We didn't tell you when Mum got ill again because –

EDDIE. You didn't.

TERRY. It was a joint decision. We knew... your mum
remembered what it had done to you before. How hard you
found it. How you found your little ways to cope.

EDDIE. My little ways to cope?

TERRY. Mum didn't need the worry of you drinking yourself to
death.

Pause.

I'm going training.

EDDIE. I know you've been going to the Edge. You've been
going to see her.

TERRY. I run. Sometimes I run up there. I admit it.

EDDIE. So you'd rather be with your dead wife than here with
your son who's still alive?

TERRY *raises his hands – 'I'm not listening to this.'*

TERRY. It happens to be where your mother's... where she's scattered. Where she loved. End of story. (*Beat*) Just because you're too scared to come with me.

EDDIE *focuses all his attention on clearing the boxes.* TERRY *is off.*

I told you to chuck that stuff. You're wasting your time.

Beat.

EDDIE. And these doctors... this Mr McNamara. He really thinks you can do the walk?

TERRY. I am doing that walk.

EDDIE. Look at you. In pain. There's nothing they can do?

TERRY. No. Why won't you believe me? It's my...

EDDIE. What?

TERRY. My... thing. Illness.

EDDIE. Disability.

TERRY. No.

EDDIE. It's fine, Dad. I don't mind sharing.

TERRY. Edward.

EDDIE (*gets out his phone*). Let's see what Dr Google says...

TERRY. There's an operation.

EDDIE*'s face lights up.*

But I'm not having it.

Exasperated, EDDIE *starts chucking everything out of the boxes and into the bin.*

EDDIE. For God's sake, Dad.

TERRY. I couldn't leave things here. I couldn't leave you.

EDDIE. So, now you care?

TERRY. That's not fair.

EDDIE. And you think it's fair not to have the operation?

TERRY. I can go on exactly as I am.

EDDIE. Your bones are crumbling away.

TERRY. So? They say Wenlock Edge is crumbling away; it's still majestic.

EDDIE. You always did have a high opinion of yourself.

TERRY. Steve Bevis came into the shop the other day –

EDDIE. I don't care about Steve Bevis.

TERRY. Went in for a routine operation, woke up on the operating table.

EDDIE. That's not going to happen.

TERRY. It happened.

EDDIE. How many operations have I had?

TERRY. That's different.

EDDIE. Mum and you just made me have them.

TERRY. We never made you. It was for the best.

EDDIE. What would Mum say now? She'd tell you to stop being so stupid.

TERRY (*beat*). You can't say that.

EDDIE. I do know she wouldn't want me to have to look after you.

TERRY. So I'm a burden?

EDDIE. I'd rather be looking after her than you.

TERRY *doesn't know what to say.* EDDIE *is vulnerable.*

If you don't have the operation. I'll be losing her all over again.

Pause.

TERRY. The consultant asked if I've done a lot of lifting and carrying? I said yes.

EDDIE. The shop. A lifetime of breaking your back hauling endless sacks of potatoes, reaching tins on shelves, constantly sweeping the front, keeping things tidy; lifting endless bags of shopping into endless boots – and for what?

TERRY. I said you. All the years I spent carrying you. All the times I lifted you.

Every time I played with you. Raised you above my head when you'd won a swimming cup or an art prize, when you did something amazing.

EDDIE. Dad, please.

TERRY. Every time I lifted you in and out of the bath, changed you, bent down to put on your socks, your shoes. I told the consultant I knew exactly why I have early onset osteoarthritis.

EDDIE *starts getting a case and chucking things in it.*

I told him straight. My condition... my disability is caused by endless years of lifting my son.

EDDIE *can't reply. He's had the words punched out of him. He wants to tell his dad to 'fuck off', but he can't.*

He just looks at TERRY *with disbelief.*

He takes his case and heads towards his bedroom. He stops. Takes the angel down from her hiding place on the mantelpiece and packs her gently. Goes to his bedroom, and shuts the door.

...

On Wenlock Edge, there is nothing, no one. Just an empty, lonely space crumbling away...

(Perhaps it feels further away than ever.)

6.

September. Lunchtime.

The flat (and its inhabitants) have eroded further. The flat shows signs of wear and tear but is certainly now more living space than stockroom.

The angel is now in pride of place.

As the scene proceeds EDDIE *should become increasingly energetic while* TERRY *gradually becomes slower and more static His trainers are still sitting unused by the door. In contrast,* EDDIE *now wears his all the time.*

TERRY *is sitting in a chair, with his foot up. He is on the phone.*

TERRY....No, I'm fine, Marina... Twisted ankle... It's bearable... what I can't bear; no, what I don't understand is why you felt the need to... I know you were being kind, but why the hell did you call Edward about my accident? I was doing fine... He was straight round – cases, the lot... True, two weeks on Darren's sofa would be enough for anyone. Now he's moved in until I'm back on my feet... He's only been here since yesterday and the little bugger's already –

The front door bangs.

That's Edward now. I thought he'd be back ages ago. Must run... Figure of speech.

He ends the call. A harassed-looking EDDIE *rushes in.*

TERRY. Had a good morning, son?

EDDIE. No. First we were out of white cobs, then we had a run on pencil cases; then to top it off a toilet paper delivery arrived just as I was closing up. We really should think about finding a more reliable supplier. (*Checks watch.*) Only fifteen minutes before I need to open up again.

I've just time to make you a sandwich, change your dressing and give you your pills. (*He goes to get them.*)

TERRY. I can take them myself.

EDDIE. I've made time in my schedule. It's fine.

TERRY. Some of that thick cut ham would be nice.

EDDIE returns with his pills and a glass of water.

EDDIE. Then Miserable Marvin came in... I know you've always said to chat to him but God... He kept going on about the roadworks by the Woodberry. And he only bought air freshener and a Twix.

TERRY. There's no harm in him.

EDDIE. Then Mrs Samuels, Mary Lacey and Susie Arthur all came in.

TERRY. Be kind to your regulars.

EDDIE. Of course, they wanted every little detail about your fall, so –

TERRY. How many times? It was not a fall.

EDDIE. I told them you were resting.

EDDIE hands TERRY the pills but he's avoiding taking them.

TERRY. I'm not old. I want you to tell everyone that I sprained my ankle. Got that? I did not 'have a fall'. It makes me sound so... elderly.

EDDIE. I told them you'd soon be sitting on your little stool, like a parrot on its perch, barking out orders. (*Of pills.*) Down in one.

TERRY (*under his breath*). Not the only one, apparently.

He makes a great performance of swallowing the pills.

Done. EDDIE efficiently starts to change TERRY's dressing.

EDDIE. By the way, Darren's getting a team together for the Bridgnorth Walk.

TERRY (*irked*). Right. Who's he doing it for?

EDDIE. Macmillan and before you say anything –

TERRY. He can't do it for them. Why can't he get his own bloody charity?

EDDIE. He wants to do it for Mum.

TERRY. But I'm – I've chosen – [Macmillan]

EDDIE. His own parents were pretty crap. He says she made him stop staring at his feet. She always loved looking up, looking out. (*Beat.*) It is a good cause.

TERRY (*still finding it hard*). Nice of him. I suppose.

EDDIE. Good. Cause I put you down as his first sponsor.

TERRY. What?!

EDDIE. After all, it's not as if you're really going to be entering now, is it? Oh, and Dad?

TERRY. Yes?

EDDIE. I'm joining Darren's team too.

TERRY. You'll never walk that far.

EDDIE. I'm not walking, Darren's borrowing a shopping trolley, and pimping it up.

TERRY (*beat*). So, everyone's doing the walk then?

EDDIE *finishes putting on the bandage and rushes to make the sandwiches.*

EDDIE. White or brown?

TERRY. Brown.

EDDIE. And you just want ham? I'm having avocado with mine.

TERRY. I like ham. You can't mess with a classic. But perhaps I'll go wild and have some piccalilli with it.

EDDIE. Actually, talking about wild ideas. I know you rejected all my previous ones but –

TERRY. Themed offers for kids? All kids want are sweets.

EDDIE. I still think we should sell more locally produced food.

TERRY. People go to the market. They come to us for essentials.

EDDIE. People want locally-grown veg, locally cured ham, and they want it now. Not just on market days.

TERRY. No. It's too expensive.

EDDIE. It would pay for itself in the long run.

TERRY. No, Eddie.

EDDIE. Okay. What about –?

TERRY. What is it about 'no' that you don't understand?

EDDIE. This one's different. I want to start a men's shed.

TERRY. What the hell is a men's shed?

EDDIE. It's a kind of talking shop.

TERRY. What are you talking about?

EDDIE. A safe space where men can come and talk about their feelings.

TERRY. Dear God. Why the hell would they want to do that?!

EDDIE. What if for one night a month it was somewhere men could bring their DIY –

TERRY. No way.

EDDIE. The idea is they all help each other with projects and as they help each other, they talk.

TERRY. We're a corner shop, not a branch of social services.

EDDIE. I really want to do this. I never want anyone to feel as lonely as I did when I first came back here.

TERRY. You're overruling me, then?

You can't just have free reign over my shop.

EDDIE. No, but what happened to not flying off the handle? Look, Dad, when I agreed to come back to look after you –

TERRY. I don't need looking after. Don't stay on my account.

EDDIE. All I want is to get you and the shop back to health again. I came back to take care of things and that's exactly what I'm going to do. Whether you like it or not. (*Beat*.) Last time... I screwed up. I'm not letting it happen again.

TERRY. Your men's shed. Give it a try. A trial.

EDDIE. Seriously?

TERRY. Yes. I suppose I should be grateful you're finally taking on more responsibility. After all, you used to just laze about.

EDDIE. I did not.

TERRY. Bet you lazed about in London too.

EDDIE. Yeah, right, with rent to pay.

TERRY. So, what about your book, your writing?

EDDIE. I've decided to use the shop as a case study.

TERRY. You're writing about the shop?

EDDIE. What better lens could there be to look at how we connect?

TERRY (*impressed and joining in*). Or how corner shops actively harness the power of social responsibility. (*Beat*.) The night you were born I had a few pints. I wanted to tell everyone down The Shakespeare. Anyway, the beer was flowing and I was... I was just so... best thing to ever happen. And I admit I'd had one too many. And I got back to the shop with Frank... You remember he used to have a flashing bowtie – he was that kind of guy. Anyway, I was so happy that night, climbed up a ladder and I painted on the shop sign –

BOTH. 'Lynham and Son'

EDDIE (*half joking*). And you got me.

Pause. The atmosphere is suddenly cold again.

TERRY. Thick cut not the breaded. (*Knowing he must keep on EDDIE's good side.*) Please, Edward.

EDDIE *exits to make the sandwiches.*

TERRY *is alone.*

...

EDDIE *is on Wenlock Edge for the first time.* (*Now it feels much closer to him but further away to* TERRY.)

He has a map on his phone. He finds the spot but can't stop. He must keep moving.

7.

Christmas Eve. Night. It's late.

The boxes are full of sellable Christmas tat. However, the flat is tastefully decorated.

Only Christmas tree lights and a desk lamp illuminate the room but EDDIE *is working, poring over the shop's accounts.*

The angel sits on top of the Christmas tree.

He is so engrossed in his work that he does not hear TERRY *as he struggles to remove his sheets from his bed. This is a huge effort.* (TERRY, *like the flat, has deteriorated significantly.*) *Unaware,* EDDIE *continues to type.*

After a while, TERRY *emerges very slowly. It is a huge effort. He is barefoot and very unsteady on his feet, holding onto everything he can. He drags the sheets, which threaten with every step to trip him up.*

He is desperately trying to be silent. This is one of the longest walks of his life.

He attempts to creep past EDDIE. *He almost makes it. Suddenly* EDDIE *looks up. They both jump!*

TERRY. Whoa!

EDDIE. Dad! What the hell are you doing?!

TERRY (*trying to hide the sheets*). You shouldn't be up this late.

EDDIE. Just checking over the accounts. We're fifteen per cent up on last year.

TERRY. Not the nodding Santas and Christmas candles? Absolute tat.

EDDIE. Tat people want to buy. (*Beat.*) What are you doing up?

TERRY. Loo. Don't let me keep you from the books, son.

EDDIE *spots the sheets.*

EDDIE. Those sheets were fresh on yesterday.

TERRY. I'll just...

EDDIE *feels the sheets – wet.*

EDDIE. You should have shouted.

TERRY. No / it's fine.

EDDIE. Let me.

TERRY. I'll take them to the machine.

EDDIE. It's no / trouble.

TERRY. No, no. I need to do things by myself.

EDDIE. They're trailing on the floor.

TERRY. I've got them.

He gathers the sheets.

Please let me do it.

EDDIE. I want to help. You might fall / again.

He gets hold of the sheets.

TERRY. No.

TERRY *lets go. He almost crumples in front of* EDDIE*'s eyes.*

Long pause.

Kindly and without any hint of embarrassment, EDDIE *takes the wet bedding out.*

TERRY *is left standing there. Helpless.*

EDDIE *returns with crisp white sheets – he puts them over the back of* TERRY*'s armchair.*

EDDIE *puts a towel down on* TERRY*'s chair. Helps him to sit.*

You'll have to put me in a nappy. We come into this world and they have to put a nappy on us. We go out of it... [the same way.]

EDDIE *pats his dad on the shoulder.*

He begins to sort the sheets. EDDIE *has them over* TERRY*'s head now.*

EDDIE. Hey, Dad. What does this remind you of?

They are both sitting under the sheet now.

TERRY. What are you doing?

EDDIE. You were always making me dens. I'd be in there reading, doodling.

TERRY. Getting up to all sorts.

EDDIE. You used to complain you wouldn't see me for days.

TERRY. Until you got hungry. But you still insisted we put your food outside your tent –

EDDIE. Den.

TERRY. Absolutely no grown ups allowed.

TERRY *makes the den properly.*

(*Beat.*) Except, you did let me in once.

EDDIE. No way. I would never have done that.

TERRY. The weekend your mum went to the Peak District.

EDDIE. Mum never went away.

TERRY. She went walking with your uncle Derek. He went walking a lot with your mum around that time.

Beat. EDDIE *almost questions further, but the moment passes.*

You were missing her. So was I. First time we'd ever been on our own.

EDDIE. Was that the weekend you smashed the teapot?

TERRY. It did it all by itself. Anyway, I helped you make a den like always. And at first I was banned from even coming near. But as the weekend went on – and things got more and more –

EDDIE. Disastrous.

TERRY. You were unsettled so on the Sunday night you invited me to dinner.

EDDIE. To dinner?!

TERRY. Yes. A whole elaborate, imaginary meal on your little plastic plates. You'd cooked it from scratch. To be honest, I think you were hungry… I hadn't been able to work the oven.

EDDIE. Now look at you, practically MasterChef.

TERRY. Anyway, when your mum did – eventually – get back, she found us asleep in your den.

Pause. They sit in the den.

Then EDDIE *whips the sheets off.*

EDDIE. Bit old for dens now.

EDDIE *begins to put fresh sheets on the bed.*

TERRY. Let me help you.

EDDIE. Don't.

TERRY (*suddenly afraid*). I've become a burden. One minute you're young, the next you turn round and you're past it. What happens to me now?

EDDIE. You're not past it. (*Beat*.) You should have shouted.

TERRY. How do you tell your son something like that? I'm not like you.

EDDIE. What do you mean?

TERRY. You spent all that time in hospital. They looked at your bits and stuff, didn't they? In some ways it must prepare you... must make you less embarrassed.

EDDIE. Unbelievable.

TERRY. I'm not like you. This is... It's all...

Pause. EDDIE swallows his annoyance.

EDDIE. Do you still need to go?

TERRY. I am not a child.

A moment. TERRY shakes his head.

Slowly TERRY rises.

You won't turn this into an anecdote, will you?

EDDIE. What?

TERRY. A funny story down The Shakespeare.

EDDIE. You really think that little of me?

TERRY. Dad pissed himself. I can just see you and Darren having a good laugh about that.

EDDIE looks upset. He continues putting sheets on the bed as TERRY shuffles painfully away. EDDIE doesn't find it easy, it is a definite wrestle, but he does it.

By the time TERRY returns – now changed – they're on.

TERRY pulls a corner off and re-tucks it.

EDDIE. Dad. [Leave it.]

TERRY. Just trying to help.

EDDIE. Leave it, will you? I'm sleeping out here. You have my bed.

TERRY. No, I'm out here. Don't make such a fuss.

EDDIE helps TERRY into bed. It is slow.

I never make a fuss.

EDDIE. Oh yeah?

TERRY. At least far less fuss than you made when… You follow your mother for that. She was always fussing about something or another – you mostly. She only ever relaxed when she was out walking.

EDDIE. Don't bring Mum into this. Don't start on her.

EDDIE's gone from caring for his dad, to now being quite rough as his hackles start to rise.

TERRY. No need to be so rough.

EDDIE. Does it even occur to you, she had caring to do, meals to prepare. Two children to look after.

TERRY. Two?

EDDIE. You're not easy, Dad. Not all of us have the time to wait while little old ladies dither over whether they want a four pack or a six pack of beans.

TERRY. We never sell six packs. Sometimes eight.

TERRY tucks his bed clothes around him and prepares for sleep.

EDDIE. I really think you enjoy running me ragged.

TERRY. Same goes for you.

EDDIE. Okay, so I need a bit of help. We both do.

It's our first Christmas here together without her. I've done everything like she did. The same decorations on the tree, even the angel.

TERRY. Wonky halo and all.

They both smile.

EDDIE. I thought we might go for a hike on top of Clee Hill tomorrow, just like the ones she used to drag us on.

TERRY *looks at him – has* EDDIE *gone mad?* EDDIE *clicks his computer – drone footage pops up.*

But from the comfort of your armchair. (*Beat.*) I even found her old bread sauce recipe.

TERRY. I hate bread sauce.

EDDIE. Me too, but you can't argue with tradition.

TERRY *settles down in bed.*

TERRY. She was our Christmas angel.

EDDIE. Yes.

They both smile.

TERRY. But she had a wonky halo too. She never wanted to let you get hurt, get damaged. She thought you'd been damaged enough already. So she kept you close, kept an eye on you, kept you safe. But I used to say, 'Let the lad run free. Let him be independent.' I knew that you could strike out on your own. I may not have been the best father in the world, but I did get that right. She was scared – and I understand why – but it's no way to live.

EDDIE *is unable to move.*

She was wonderful. But she wasn't perfect. (*Beat.*) None of us are.

TERRY *checks his watch.*

It's one minute past midnight. Happy Christmas, Eddie.

EDDIE *wants to say so much, but he can't.*

...

It's snowing on Wenlock Edge. EDDIE *comes to the spot. He stops.*

He lets the snow envelope him for a while.

Meanwhile, the Edge creeps ever closer to the flat...

8.

March.

TERRY *lies on the floor; he's been there a while.*

Pause.

EDDIE *comes in from training.*

TERRY. I was beginning to think you weren't ever coming back.

EDDIE. Why didn't you call me?!

TERRY. Mobile's in my coat pocket.

EDDIE. How many times? Keep it / on you.

TERRY. Get me up.

> *They try but it's too hard.*

> EDDIE *uses all his body strength but it's not working.*

EDDIE. Have you broken anything?

TERRY (*shakes his head*). I need the toilet.

EDDIE. I'm doing my best.

TERRY. I've been holding it in for a while.

EDDIE. Okay, okay.

TERRY. It's urgent.

EDDIE. What happened?

TERRY. Nothing. I tripped.

EDDIE. Can you crawl? To the toilet?

TERRY. I don't know.

EDDIE. Maybe then you can lever yourself up? On the seat.

TERRY. If I can't do it here, then I won't be able to do / it there, will I?

EDDIE. It was just an idea.

TERRY. Well, come up with something better. Where were you?

EDDIE. Training. Ten of us now.

TERRY (*beat*). No chance of me doing it now.

EDDIE. Always next year.

TERRY. But I wanted to… Her memory.

EDDIE *gets his phone out.*

Who are you calling?

EDDIE. An ambulance.

TERRY (*takes the phone from him*). No ambulance. It'll take forever to get here. Try again.

EDDIE. I'm not strong enough.

TERRY. Again.

EDDIE. Dad.

TERRY. I believe in you.

EDDIE. It's not belief I need.

They do. No good.

EDDIE *looks surprised.*

They try again. It works. Finally, although shaken, TERRY *is on a chair.*

TERRY. I'm ill.

EDDIE. Don't you mean 'handicapped'?

This time TERRY *feels the weight of the word. He looks ashamed.*

TERRY. I was… I was wrong. I'm sorry. Still doesn't mean I'm comfortable with the word.

EDDIE. What word? Disabled?

TERRY. Maybe I don't need a word. Just give me time.

EDDIE. I still think you should be checked out.

TERRY. No.

EDDIE. You're so stubborn.

TERRY. They'll separate us.

EDDIE. No they won't.

TERRY. I know what happens. They'll put us in a home.

EDDIE. Well, it's not happening to me.

TERRY. Your mum and me, we fought so hard to keep you out of those places. The system.

EDDIE. I'm not going to let it happen to you, either.

TERRY. You might not have a choice.

EDDIE. I stayed to look after you. We had a deal. And part of that is you don't die. But this… It's getting worse. If you'd just reconsider having the operation.

TERRY. I'm booked in for the fourteenth of next month.

Beat.

EDDIE (*consulting the calendar*). I'll have to get cover for the shop.

TERRY. No you won't.

EDDIE. I'm coming with you.

TERRY. I said no.

EDDIE. Now you're just being ridiculous.

TERRY. Marina's volunteered to take me.

EDDIE. I see.

TERRY. She offered. There's no need to look at me like that?

EDDIE. I'm not looking at you like anything.

TERRY. Saves putting you out, organising taxis, et cetera, et cetera.

EDDIE (*beat*). It was her. She changed your mind about the operation.

TERRY. It was my decision. It's what I want.

EDDIE. Good.

TERRY. Marina just pointed out the benefits. We had a glass of wine –

EDDIE. You shouldn't drink wine, it's bad for your joints.

TERRY. – and she listened. To my side. My concerns.

EDDIE. How serious is this, Dad? This relationship?

TERRY. We're just friends.

EDDIE. Just friends? It seems like she can get you to do the impossible. The full three-sixty.

TERRY. She just… she got it, okay? I know you think it's a great joke to tease me, but there's nothing in it.

EDDIE. Thing is, Dad, I wouldn't mind if there was.

TERRY. Just a bit of company, that's all. She / understands.

EDDIE. Good.

TERRY. One… one able-bodied… person to another.

Silence.

EDDIE. Perhaps I'll book myself a little holiday while you're recuperating. As Mrs Henderson is so keen to look after you.

TERRY. I'll be coming back here after I'm discharged. Wouldn't want to put Marina out.

EDDIE. I sometimes think you get some perverted kick out of driving me up the wall.

TERRY. You are family. What do you expect?

EDDIE. Do you know how much care you're going to need? Where am I meant to find the time?

TERRY. Hold on. You've changed your tune. A minute ago you were all for looking after me…

EDDIE. Five minutes ago you weren't having it. (*Beat.*) Of course I'll look after you.

TERRY (*beat*). I'm not trying to replace your mum.

EDDIE. I know.

TERRY. Honest.

EDDIE. It's fine.

TERRY. But maybe there is a bit more to it. With Marina.

EDDIE (*grins and punches the air*). Yes.

TERRY. There's no need to go overboard.

EDDIE. Darren owes me a fiver.

TERRY. You put a bet on / me?

EDDIE. He said you'd never admit it.

He starts texting.

What a glorious day.

TERRY. We could get someone in. A carer. Like you had at uni.

EDDIE. And you'd be okay with that?

TERRY. Someone we pay. Privately.

EDDIE. But the money?

TERRY. Rainy day fund.

EDDIE. But that seems so…

TERRY. It might not be full on pouring but…

EDDIE. It feels like giving up.

TERRY. Will you come with me to the hospital?

EDDIE *nods. A shared moment of warmth.*

I held your finger in the incubator when you were a baby.

EDDIE (*beat*). I'd better grab a shower.

TERRY. I wanted to do the walk for her, you know.

EDDIE (*nods*). Let me do it for both of you. My apology. I should have been here for her. I should have been brave like you.

Pause.

TERRY. They wheeled her into hospital and I never saw her again.

EDDIE *reaches out to touch his dad's hand. Doesn't quite make it.*

The lights fade.

...

The sun comes out on Wenlock Edge as EDDIE *trains, hard.*

Meanwhile, the Edge seems to be creeping even closer...

9.

The day of the Bridgnorth Walk.

The boxes are full of Easter eggs again.

EDDIE *and* TERRY *dash in.* EDDIE *is triumphant, sporting a medal.*

TERRY *is a full month into recovery.*

TERRY. You were amazing, son. The whole team.

EDDIE. And we didn't lose anyone on the way.

TERRY. You all looked so... It was brilliant. The only thing that would have made it even better –

EDDIE. Next year. Time to change your dressing.

TERRY *gets seated while* EDDIE *finds the dressings.*
TERRY *removes his shirt and* EDDIE *expertly cleans and dresses the wound on* TERRY*'s spine.*

TERRY. How's she doing then?

EDDIE. Coming on.

TERRY. Good, good.

EDDIE. She's still got a way to go.

TERRY. Shouldn't have stood up so long, talking.

EDDIE. It was great to see you more your old self.

TERRY. You should go and celebrate. You didn't need to come home with me.

EDDIE. I had this email yesterday from my supervisor. He's recommending my work for publication.

EDDIE already has his phone out. Passes it to TERRY.

TERRY (bursting with pride). That's great, son. It's... great.

They almost hug but don't quite make it. TERRY *gives him his phone back.*

EDDIE. Always thinking you can go one better, eh, Dad?

TERRY. I've been thinking about the shop... selling up. I've spoken to a couple of agents.

EDDIE. No. You can't.

TERRY. Not straight away, but there's already been some interest.

EDDIE. We're making a profit, we're picking up trade.

TERRY. Yeah and it's great. But this – (*Indicating* EDDIE's *phone.*)

EDDIE. Changes nothing.

TERRY. I can't run the shop any more.

EDDIE. You'll be back to normal soon.

TERRY. Be sensible, Edward. We both know I've been kidding myself for a long time. You never wanted to be a shopkeeper. That was my dream.

You're going to be published.

EDDIE. And what will I do? Become some crusty academic?

TERRY. You can do whatever you want.

EDDIE. I kept it going for you. Lynham and Son, the sign says.

TERRY. Eddie, no.

EDDIE. All the memories.

TERRY. It's time to make some new ones. Plus, I'll take all the good ones with me. (*Beat*.) Marina – Mrs Henderson and I... If I sold up we could pool our resources and live very comfortably in her cottage in Barmouth.

EDDIE. Oh.

TERRY. Nothing's settled.

EDDIE. Is she forcing you?

TERRY. Of course not.

EDDIE. That business is made of your sweat, your heart. (*Beat*.) I've found my place.

TERRY. But it's time to move on. (*Beat*.) Marina was so kind when I was in hospital, bringing me food, checking in on me, bringing endless bunches of grapes.

EDDIE. Just because a woman brings you grapes doesn't mean you have to sell up and move to the seaside with her?

TERRY. We got close. Closer. (*Beat*.) You won't go without.

EDDIE. Do you really think I give a monkey's about money now?

TERRY. If I don't do it now I'll...

EDDIE. What, Dad?

TERRY. At the moment I've a chance to leave while it's my choice. Before I'm ground into the shop floor. Your mother never got that choice.

Beat.

I saw your face when you showed me that email. You have a real chance. Take it.

EDDIE. I was so scared to come home but now I know exactly what it feels like. I want to stay.

TERRY. It's time.

EDDIE. We can't…

Why the rush? Did you plan this?

TERRY (*shakes his head*). *When* I saw you cross the finish line this afternoon; the relief and the joy on your face… Finally. I knew… I know… we have to let her go.

EDDIE. I can't.

EDDIE *stands in the middle of the space and carefully carries the angel down from the mantelpiece, with shaking hands.*

They don't notice as Wenlock Edge begins to creep into the corners of the room…

Wenlock Edge is climbing the walls now…

Now, are they on the Edge or in the flat?

EDDIE *stands on the edge…*

Come to the edge.

We might fall.

Come to the edge.

It's too high!

COME TO THE EDGE!

And they came,

and he pushed,

And they flew.

Does he fall or does he fly?

Blackout.

A Nick Hern Book

Little Bits of Ruined Beauty first published in Great Britain as a paperback original in 2022 by Nick Hern Books Limited, The Glasshouse, 49a Goldhawk Road, London W12 8QP, in association with Pentabus

Litte Bits of Ruined Beauty copyright © 2022 Tom Wentworth

The poem 'Come to the Edge' copyright © Christopher Logue, reprinted with permission of David Godwin Associates Ltd

Tom Wenworth has asserted his right to be identified as the author of this work

Cover image by Stephen Long

Designed and typeset by Nick Hern Books, London
Printed in Great Britain by Mimeo Ltd, Huntingdon, Cambridgeshire PE29 6XX

A CIP catalogue record for this book is available from the British Library

ISBN 978 1 83904 128 0